The North American
Beaver

Returning Wildlife

The North American
Beaver

John E. Becker

KIDHAVEN PRESS

THOMSON

★

GALE

Detroit • New York • San Diego • San Francisco
Boston • New Haven, Conn. • Waterville, Maine
London • Munich

To my son, John, who has believed in his dad
every step of the way

Library of Congress Cataloging-in-Publication Data

Becker, John E., 1942–
  The North American beaver / by John E. Becker.
    p. cm. — (Returning wildlife)
  Includes bibliographical references (p.   ).
Summary: Discusses the history of beaver trapping and the fur trade, the
near extinction of the species, the beaver's habits and habitat, and
conservation efforts leading to the beaver's comeback.
  ISBN 0-7377-1011-X (hardcover: alk. paper)
  1. American beaver—Juvenile literature. 2. Endangered species—
North America—Juvenile literature. 3. Wildlife conservation—
North America—Juvenile literature. [1. American beaver. 2. Beavers.
3. Endangered species. 4. Wildlife conservation.] I. Title. II. Series.
  QL737 .R632 B44 2002
  599.37—dc21

2001002212

Copyright 2002 by KidHaven Press,
an imprint of The Gale Group
10911 Technology Place, San Diego, California 92127

Contents

chapter 1

Beavers and the New World

Beavers are among nature's most industrious animals, building **dams, lodges, canals**, and dens. By damming streams, beavers create homes for other animals and provide a cleaner environment. No other animal, except man, is so capable of altering its surroundings.

Generally, beavers try to avoid contact with people. Yet few animals have had more of an effect on human history. The beaver's soft, brown fur was the reason that North America was explored and settled by Europeans. Before Europeans came to the New World, more than 60 million beavers roamed the wilds of North America.

Soon after Christopher Columbus discovered America in 1492, Europeans began trading with the native Indians for beaver skins. They later hunted the animals themselves to supply the furs needed for fashionable clothes and hats in Europe and Asia.

Hundreds of thousands of beavers were killed in North America from the middle of the sixteenth to the middle of the nineteenth century. By the end of that period, beavers were almost completely gone from their former range in the United States.

A change in fashion from beaver felt to hats and clothing made of silk may have saved beavers from extinction. As the nineteenth century drew to a close, people also began to recognize that beavers were worthy of being protected. Laws making it illegal to kill beavers were passed at that time. Those laws allowed

Native Americans deliver beaver skins to European traders.

beavers to begin increasing their numbers once again. When they were relocated to areas from which they had disappeared, beavers began expanding their territory and reproducing rapidly.

Today beavers are found in almost every area that they once occupied. Unfortunately, their building ability can work against them. When dams flood highways, farms, golf courses, and other property, beavers are considered pests. So people are now challenged to deal with beavers in ways that will not send them toward extinction again.

Nature's Great Builders

Beavers have been on earth for at least 35 million years. One giant ancestor of today's beavers, **Castorides**,

7

A *Castor fiber* beaver munches on tasty greenery.

lived in North America. It was as big as a black bear and weighed over five hundred pounds. Today only two species of beavers exist, **Castor fiber** in Europe and Asia and **Castor canadensis** in Canada, the United States, and Mexico.

Beavers belong to the **rodent** family (order Rodentia). They are the second largest rodents after the **capybara** of South America. Newborn beavers, called **kits**, generally weigh about one pound when they are born. They continue to grow throughout their lifetime. Adult beavers may weigh more than sixty pounds. A few have exceeded a hundred pounds.

Beavers are skillful builders. When a beaver family moves into an area with a slow-moving stream, they immediately set about cutting down trees. To do this, a beaver stands on its hind legs. Using its tail as a prop and its extremely sharp front (**incisor**) teeth as an ax, a beaver can cut through the trunk of a tree in amazingly short time. A single beaver can gnaw through a tree six inches thick in ten to twenty minutes.

A sturdy tree is no match for this beaver's sharp teeth.

Once the tree falls, the beaver cuts the trunk and branches into smaller pieces that it drags to the stream. When the pieces are far from water, beavers use the strong nails on their front paws to dig canals in which they can float tree branches. They swim these logs out to the site where the dam will be. Next, beavers wedge these limbs in the stream bottom, piecing these together with rocks and mud. When the structure is finished, the flow of water is stopped, creating a pond behind the dam.

Beavers continually add to the dam to keep the water trapped in the pond. They also make repairs with sticks and mud. While dams of three hundred feet are not uncommon, a few have been recorded as long as a thousand feet.

Once the dam has been finished, the beavers build a home, known as a lodge, of sticks and mud. The lodge has at least two escape tunnels that open into the water and an opening at the top for ventilation. Beaver lodges may rise as high as ten feet from the bottom of the pond. The largest beaver lodge recorded was sixteen feet high and forty-five feet across. Because beaver lodges are not difficult to find, beavers are much easier to locate and kill than other rodents.

Beaver Behaviors

Beavers' main diet consists of leaves, bark, and twigs. A beaver may eat up to two pounds of food a day. To their favorite trees of aspen, cottonwood, and willow, they add water lilies, skunk cabbage, sedge grasses, and other water plants. They store branches stuck in the bottom of the pond for a winter food supply called a **cache**.

While beavers look awkward waddling about on land, they are ideally built for life in the water. Their torpedo-like shape helps them to glide through the

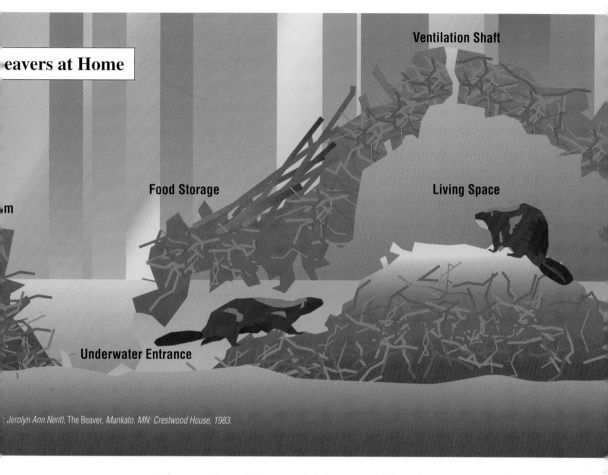

Ventilation Shaft

eavers at Home

Food Storage

.m

Living Space

Underwater Entrance

: Jerolyn Ann Nentl, The Beaver, Mankato, MN: Crestwood House, 1983.

water. A beaver's tail is used like a rudder for steering, as well as for a quick burst of speed when needed. They have large, webbed back feet and almost handlike front feet that allow them to grasp tree branches.

Beavers have flaps behind their front teeth to keep water out of their throats when they swim underwater. They also have valves that close their ears and noses and a clear membrane that covers their eyes so they can see underwater.

Beavers can stay submerged for up to fifteen minutes. Since beaver lungs are more efficient than human lungs, a beaver gets as much as 50 percent more oxygen per breath than a person. Beavers also channel

The beaver's webbed back feet are powerful swimming and grasping tools.

more oxygen to their brains and less to their legs when they are underwater.

While beavers do not have particularly good vision, they have well-developed senses of hearing and smelling. If they are alarmed while in the water, beavers will slap the water with their tails. The resulting sound warns other beavers that danger is near.

Wetlands Developers

Wetlands are important to the environment. Because beavers are nature's wetlands developers they help to offset the loss of wetlands destroyed by man.

When beavers build their dams, they flood an area behind the dam that then becomes a shallow pond. As the waters of the pond spread out, the surrounding trees die off. Before long, water plants such as water lilies and cattails take hold. Muskrats make houses in the reeds. Frogs and turtles find shelter and food along the banks of the pond. Many other animals such as deer, fox, and bear come to the pond for a drink of water.

As time goes by, fish become more numerous. Even sport fish, which could not survive the cold waters of a mountain stream, flourish in wetlands created by the beavers. When fish are abundant, otters, eagles, and wading birds like cranes and egrets come to the pond. The sounds of ducks and geese fill the air as the pond becomes their home as well. Eventually, the beavers will have established an entire ecological community that survives because of their hard work.

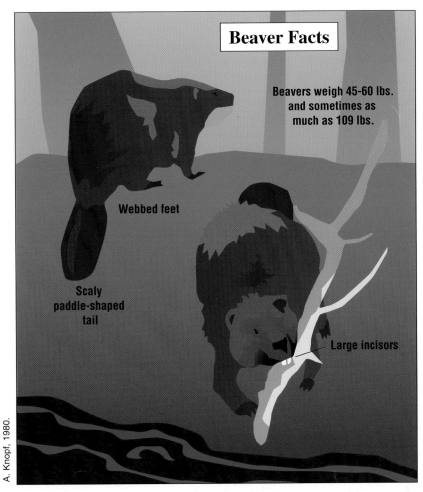

Beaver Facts

Beavers weigh 45-60 lbs. and sometimes as much as 109 lbs.

Webbed feet

Scaly paddle-shaped tail

Large incisors

Source: John O. Whitaker, Jr., *The Audubon Society Field Guide to North American Mammals*, New York: Alfred A. Knopf, 1980.

A beaver shows off its huge front teeth.

Why People Hunt Beavers

People hunted beavers for various reasons. Near the base of a beaver's tail are **glands** that secrete a scented fluid. Beavers use this to mark their territory and water-proof their fur. Both Europeans and North American Indians prized the fluid, known as **castoreum**, as a medicine to treat a variety of ailments, including rheumatism, headache, arthritis, and fever. Europeans also use cas-toreum as an important ingredient in certain perfumes.

Through the centuries, people have also eaten beavers. Native Americans regularly ate beaver. They especially enjoyed the beaver's tail, which was eaten as a delicacy.

Beaver Fur

What people find most attractive about the beaver, however, is its fur. Beavers actually have two fur coats. The outer coat consists of long, coarse guard hairs that are quite large in diameter. These protect the thickly matted hairs underneath known as underfur. When brushed into a fine felt, the underfur has a luxuriant softness that caused beavers to be hunted for their fur in Europe for centuries.

In the Middle Ages, wealthy people in Europe wore the furs of wild animals for warmth and as a sign of their social rank. As time passed, more and more people earned incomes that allowed them to buy clothing made of furs. Therefore, the demand for furs increased steadily.

The extremely high quality of beaver fur made it perfect for the tall felt gentlemen's hats known as beavers that became popular across Europe. Consequently, many beavers disappeared, first from Europe and then from Asia. But explorers soon discovered that North America had a seemingly endless supply.

chapter 2

New World Fur Trade

In North America early European explorers found native Indians eager to trade beaver skins, which they had in abundance, for knives, axes, guns, and other products made of iron. Soon there was a brisk trade between the Indians and the newcomers. Beaver pelts were such a common trade item that they were used as a type of currency with which other items could be purchased. The French and Dutch were particularly interested in trading with the Indians.

Beavers in Trade

Shortly after they arrived in the New World, the French established trading centers to which the Indians brought the furs of beavers. In 1581 French merchants sent a single ship to America to transport furs back to France. The profits from that voyage were so great that in 1583 they sent three more ships. That venture proved so successful that five ships sailed across the Atlantic in 1584. Ten more were needed for all the furs shipped in 1585. By the latter part of the sixteenth century, French ships regularly sailed to the New World to collect the furs of beavers.

In 1624 the Dutch West India Company exported 400 beaver and 700 otter skins from New Amsterdam (New York City). By 1635 that number increased to 14,891 beaver and 1,413 otter skins. In the ten-year period from 1626 to 1635, the total number of skins exported from New Amsterdam totaled 80,183 beavers

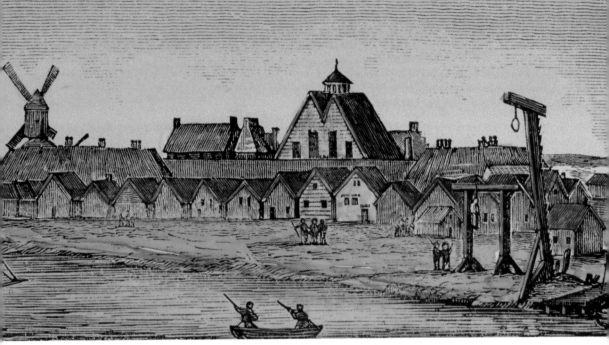

The Dutch West India Company made huge profits by exporting beaver and otter skins from New Amsterdam (pictured).

and 7,347 otters. The Dutch West India Company steadily increased its trade in skins until 1664 when beaver pelts were worth about $2.25.

About that time the English, who were rivals of the French and Dutch, became more deeply involved in the North American **fur trade**. After the English took over the territory previously held by the Dutch, they began an aggressive campaign to gain control of the fur trade from the French. Thereafter, Indian and European trappers began scouring the remotest areas of North America to find beavers. By the middle of the seventeenth century, English and French ships were regularly sailing between North America and England, France, Spain, and Italy. Those ships were filled with the furs of beavers and many other animals.

Under English rule, beavers were considered so important to New York that they were shown as the central symbol of the area's seal. By 1687, however, the governor of New York was complaining that the number of

Ships leave France for North America, where they will buy animal skins.

beavers sent to England had dropped from an average of between 35,000 and 40,000 to only 9,000.

Beaver pelts continued to be the chief export of New York until 1700. But in that year, the new governor of the province reported that the trade in beaver pelts had fallen dramatically. In both New York and Boston, fur exports had declined to the point that it was hardly worth the price of transporting the skins. After that time the number of beaver skins shipped to England declined rapidly. Within a few years the trade in beaver skins ended altogether in New York, as the beavers were nearly extinct in the area. Substantial numbers of beaver skins were still being exported from New England, Delaware, Maryland, Pennsylvania, and Virginia, however. But just a few years later, the trade in beaver skins stopped in those areas as well because of over-hunting.

Conflict in the New World

Throughout the seventeenth and into the eighteenth century, bitter fighting broke out between the French and English over fur trading and other matters. When war between the two countries began in Europe, the conflict spilled over to North America. The battles in North America, known as the French and Indian War, were fought from 1754 to 1763. In the end England defeated France and claimed all of the territory east of

An artist vividly depicts a battle scene from the French and Indian War.

the Mississippi River as its own. With the war over, England went back to exporting fur, as the demand for North American beavers had not lessened.

By the time of the American Revolution, beavers were gone from much of the area of the original thirteen colonies. After the war there was a great deal of interest in the exploration of the land stretching westward from Pennsylvania. Locating new sources of beaver was a major priority for the early explorers and trappers.

Beginning of the End

When President Thomas Jefferson completed the Louisiana Purchase from France in 1803, a vast new area west of the Mississippi River was open to exploration and trade. That new territory was rich with beaver. After Lewis and Clark explored the area from 1804 to 1806 and published what they had found, a determined search for beaver began.

Two companies—Hudson's Bay Company, operating out of Canada, and the American Fur Company, headed by American millionaire John Jacob Astor—took a heavy toll on beavers. The two companies tried to beat each other in getting more furs, causing beavers to disappear more rapidly. Beavers were soon gone from the middle of the continent.

Another fashion-related development added to beavers disappearing at that time. Beau Brummel, an Englishman known as a fashion trend-

These dapper nineteenth-century gentlemen are wearing beaver hats.

setter, popularized a hat known as the gray beaver. The gray beaver was a tall top hat, gray in color, with a curled brim. Soon more beavers were being taken than ever.

An invention by an American proved to be the final blow for beavers in North America, however. In 1823 an American, Sewell Newhouse, developed a lightweight steel trap that far surpassed other traps manufactured prior to that time. These extremely efficient devices contributed greatly to the demise of the beaver. Thereafter, trappers were able to capture greater numbers of beaver at one time.

Frontier naturalist John James Audubon in his book, *Audbon's Quadrupeds of North America,* described the success the trappers had in the early part of the nineteenth century capturing beavers:

> A good trapper used to catch about eighty beavers in the autumn, sixty or seventy in the spring, and upwards of three hundred in the summer in the mountains; taking occasionally as many as five hundred in one year. Sixty, or seventy, beaver skins are required to make a pack weighing one hundred pounds; which, when sent to a good market, is worth, even now, from three to four hundred dollars.

The fur trade in the American Northwest produced the legendary "mountain men." These bearded, buckskin-clad adventurers took huge numbers of beaver from the last great stronghold for them in North America. The Rocky Mountain Fur Company, for example, trapped over forty thousand beavers, with a value of $250,000, from the Rocky Mountain area between 1823 and 1827. At that time beaver pelts were selling for approximately $3 each. As many as six different companies were

Mountain men made huge profits by trapping thousands of beavers and selling their skins.

combing the Rocky Mountains, with hundreds of trappers to exhaust the supply of beavers.

Clinging to Existence

The fur trade had reduced beaver populations in the United States to such low numbers that many people feared they would never recover. A few people, however, believed that with help beavers could make a comeback. But much would need to be done before beavers could return to their natural habitats across the continent.

Beaver Comeback

It has been estimated that at the time the first Europeans landed in North America, beavers numbered more than 60 million. But as early as 1634, French Jesuit priests felt it necessary to instruct the Indians in the benefits of not killing all the beavers that they located. They counseled them not to take the younger, smaller beavers out of a lodge so those animals might one day repopulate the area.

Unfortunately, the Jesuits' advice was ignored in most instances when beavers were discovered. The generally accepted practice was to kill every beaver found in an area and then move on to new territory until all the beavers were gone from that area as well. It must have seemed to the fur trappers and settlers that beavers were so plentiful that the supply would never run out. Gradually, however, beavers were eliminated from one section of the country after another. Then, just as it appeared that beavers might completely disappear from America, a change in fashion saved them from extinction.

A Glimmer of Hope

After three hundred years of being hunted, North American beavers finally received relief from being killed for their fur in the 1840s. In 1840 a hatter's apprentice in London discovered that hats made with finely combed silk had a far greater shine than those of beaver felt. That discovery, and the extremely low numbers of

French Jesuit priests tried to convince the Indians that it was beneficial not to kill every beaver they found.

beavers remaining in their natural range, all but ended the beaver-trapping era in the United States.

Beavers, thereafter, were considered rare, and the mountain men who had hunted beavers so relentlessly became scouts for the army or guides for wagon trains carrying settlers west. In Canada the government-controlled Hudson's Bay Company took measures to see that beavers were not overhunted. Consequently, that country continued trapping beavers and traded 3 million beaver skins between 1853 and 1877.

Beaver Conservation Begins

Toward the end of the nineteenth century, people began to realize that beavers were disappearing. Small groups of beavers could still be found in places like the Rocky Mountains and the mountains of the Pacific coast. Fortunately for the beavers, a growing number of people believed that steps should be taken to prevent beavers from becoming extinct.

In the 1840s, beavers were able to live more peacefully as trapping diminished.

Beaver fur was in demand for fashionable coats and other clothing in the late 1800s.

In 1877 Missouri gave beavers legal protection. In 1885 Maine did the same, followed by Colorado in 1899. The first few steps had been taken to prevent the disappearance of beavers in North America, but the question remained, "Could beavers be brought back?"

Despite laws to protect them, beavers continued to disappear during the latter part of the nineteenth century. Beaver fur was not in demand for hats, but there continued to be an interest in beaver fur for coats and other garments. Beavers were killed wherever they were found.

Yet another problem for beavers was the loss of woodlands to settlement and logging interests. With the clearing of trees from vast areas of the eastern and central portions of the United States, beavers simply had very few places to construct dams and lodges.

Beavers seemed to be headed toward extinction, but then a historic event gave them another chance. In 1872 President Ulysses S. Grant signed into law a bill that created Yellowstone National Park. This, the first national park in the United States, also became a 3,472-square-mile wildlife sanctuary.

Yellowstone, in time, would become a safe place for beavers, as well as grizzly bears, elk, moose, bison, trumpeter swans, and many other species of wild animals. Yellowstone was also the first national park established anywhere in the world, and its opening signaled a new appreciation by people for the natural environment.

Merely setting aside land does not, however, ensure that the wildlife within its boundaries is safe. For the first several years of Yellowstone's existence as a park, poaching of the animals within the park was common. In 1886 the secretary of the interior decided that the U.S. Army needed to be called in to prevent poaching

National parks have become a haven for beavers and other wildlife.

and maintain order in the park. The army patrolled the park for the next thirty years.

Once the park was truly protected, beavers became the first species to establish themselves. As the years passed, more visitors came to Yellowstone from all over the United States and other countries around the world. Those visitors told park officials that one of their favorite activities was to watch the beavers build their dams and lodges.

A New Century

By the dawn of the twentieth century, North American beavers were still clinging to survival. It was estimated that by 1900 only 100,000 beavers remained in all of North America. People who were eager to see beavers become reestablished across the country were encouraged by two important factors. First, beavers' natural predators, such as wolves, cougars, and bears, were no longer a threat to the beavers because they, too, were in very low numbers. And trees, like aspens and willows, were returning to large areas from which they had disappeared. These elements were important for beavers to come back.

In 1901 President William McKinley created the 59,020-acre Wichita Mountains Forest Preserve. Eight thousand acres in the preserve became one of the first national wildlife refuges in the United States when President Theodore Roosevelt signed a presidential proclamation in 1905. The purpose of the refuge was to protect the few remaining plains bison, but it also provided another area where beavers could live out their lives in relative security.

New York Leads the Way

It has been estimated that as many as 3 million beavers lived in New York at the beginning of the seventeenth

Beavers can flourish in the peaceful Wichita Mountains Forest Preserve, seen here.

century. By 1800 that number had been reduced to five thousand beavers and was down to no more than three hundred by 1840. As the nineteenth century drew to a close, only one colony of five beavers was known to survive in New York.

With the beginning of the twentieth century came a growing national awareness of the need to conserve wildlife resources. That concern was mirrored in New York. In 1895 the Fisheries, Game and Forest Law made it clear that beavers were not to be caught or killed in that state. From 1901 to 1907, a total of thirty-four beavers were released in the Adirondack Mountains region of New York. Fourteen of those beavers came from Yellowstone National Park. Because they were protected, the beavers quickly multiplied. By 1907 it was estimated that a hundred beavers were once again living in New York.

After that, beavers increased so rapidly that by 1915 about fifteen thousand lived in the Adirondack region alone. With the increase in beaver populations

Modern-day beavers enjoy the benefits of wildlife conservation.

came a sharp increase in complaints about damage caused by flooding from beaver dams. Despite the re-institution of a trapping season for beavers in New York, they have steadily increased in numbers. Today about seventy thousand beavers live in the state of New York.

Beavers Come Home

By 1913 a total of twenty-four states and Canada had passed laws to protect beavers from trapping. California followed New York's lead and began returning beavers in 1924. Missouri followed New York and California and began bringing them back in 1928. By 1940 sixty-four beavers had been transferred to West Virginia from Michigan and Wisconsin. To return beavers to remote areas of Idaho and Colorado, wildlife officials parachuted the animals in wooden crates that opened on impact. Beavers were now back, but could they avoid conflicts with people in their new surroundings?

chapter 4

A Hopeful Future

When the phone rang at the Ohio Department of Natural Resources, Division of Wildlife, office wildlife biologist Dan Huss answered the call.

"Is this the right place to call if I have a beaver complaint?" came an angry voice from the other end of the line.

"Yes, sir," Dan answered politely.

"Well, I want to know what I can do about these beavers and the damage they did when they dammed our stream," the caller said.

"What exactly did they damage?" Dan asked.

"Why, those pests have destroyed just about everything they've come in contact with! We used to have lots of beautiful aspen trees that lined the stream at the edge of our property. They're gone now—just stumps left to show where they were. It'll cost a fortune to replace them!"

"I'm sorry about the damage that's been done, and I understand what you're going through," Dan replied.

"Being sorry won't replace those trees, or unplug our sewer lines, or get the water out of our basement. And now part of our driveway has collapsed!"

No Easy Answer

There is no question that beavers have made a comeback across the country. They can now be found in almost every area that they once called home. Millions of beavers once again roam across North America.

Some people are angry at the destruction caused when beavers cut down trees.

While the return of beavers has been praised by conservation-minded individuals as a major success story, not everyone is excited to see beavers living near-by. As the beaver populations continue to grow each year, the number of beaver-related problems increase as

33

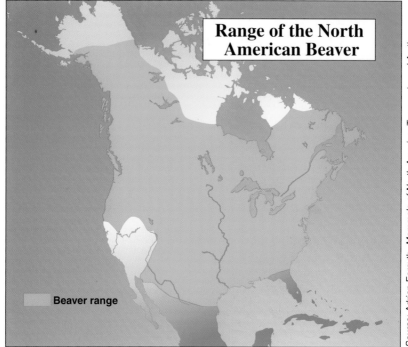

Range of the North American Beaver

Beaver range

Source: Adrian Forsyth, *Mammals of North America: Temperate and Arctic Regions*, Buffalo: Firefly Books, 1999.

well. As early as the mid-1950s, several states had already opened trapping seasons in response to beaver-related complaints.

Damage to farmland, trees, golf courses, roadways, and homes now run into the millions of dollars each year. Many people are not tolerant of beavers at all and are insistent that the beavers must be removed. In some instances, removal means live-trapping the animals and locating them in areas where their damming activities cannot damage valuable property. In many cases, however, the solution has been to kill the beavers.

Beaver Problems in New York

Since New York was the first state to begin **reintroducing** beavers in 1901 they were also one of the first states to have problems with reintroduced beavers. New York's experience has been typical of the problems experienced by other states where beavers have returned.

As beavers grew in numbers, they quickly came into conflict with landowners. By 1913 problems associated with beavers had become so numerous that a legalized trapping season was considered to cope with the problem.

In 1915 permits were occasionally issued by the state to dynamite beaver dams and lodges. The next year the state of New York began granting permits to people so they could remove problem beavers. Legal trapping of beavers (from March 1 to March 31) was allowed in parts of New York for the first time in twenty-nine years in 1924.

Public sentiment shifted back and forth on the beaver issue over the ensuing years. Strong sentiment in favor of beaver conservation gave way to demands for more liberal trapping seasons. Therefore, over the next thirty years, New York both opened and then closed beaver trapping. In 1955 a statewide trapping season was instituted in New York for the first time in the twentieth century.

By the late 1960s, New York Conservation Department officials recognized that beavers benefited the environment by creating wetlands across the state.

A beaver in its pond. Ponds formed by beaver dams create wetlands that help the environment.

Since that time a policy of beaver management, based on the benefits they provide, has been in effect in New York.

Value of Beaver Ponds

Beaver ponds provide a great many benefits to the surrounding countryside. By acting as a catch basin for rainwater and runoff, beaver ponds help to conserve water, raise the underground water table, and reduce

A young cougar confronts a beaver in its icy pond. The pond serves as a catch basin for rain.

the effects of flooding. When they have been reintro-duced to dry, barren land beavers have transformed that land into a healthy, green wetland environment.

Wetlands filter pollutants out of the water. Danger-ous chemicals gradually settle to the bottom. There they are absorbed by the roots of wetland plants like water hyacinths and duckweed and trapped in the soggy mud. Wetlands also trap tiny organisms that can cause diseases.

Water quality improves when beaver ponds slow the rate at which water flows. This causes **silt** to settle to the bottom of the pond rather than be carried down-stream. Beaver dams help prevent soil erosion because the water that flows from the dam is slow moving. Stream banks near a beaver dam do not erode as they did before the dam was created.

Once beavers have exhausted the supply of trees around their pond, they will move on and build a dam on another stream. The old dam will gradually break down. The water will flow out of the dam, and a lush, soil-rich meadow will remain. That meadow becomes home to yet another unique ecosystem for plants and animals.

Helping Hand for Beavers

Many people across the United States are working to help beavers and people live together peacefully. One of the most effective ways to do that is to install devices to minimize or eliminate the damage caused by beavers.

One organization in Colorado, Wildlife 2000, is work-ing to deal with beaver problems in positive ways. One solution to the problem has come in the form of wrap-ping trees with wire to prevent beavers from destroying them. "Beaver deceivers," wire fences built at the entrance to culverts that prevent beavers from clogging the culverts, are another solution. And when necessary, Wildlife 2000 has live-trapped and then relocated "problem" beavers.

A young member of Wildlife 2000 live-traps a beaver, which will be moved to a safer location.

An industrious beaver adds to its dam. It is up to people to ensure that beavers continue to exist in healthy numbers.

Prospects for the Future

Beavers are back. Across the country beavers are either already firmly reestablished or are in the process of settling back into their former habitats. Whether or not they disappear again will depend on concerned people finding ways for them to peacefully coexist with property owners. If that can be accomplished, beavers should be with us forever.

cache: A place where food is stored.

canal: A ditch dug into the ground in which water flows.

capybara: The world's largest rodent, weighing over one hundred pounds.

castoreum: An oily substance produced by glands located near the tail of a beaver.

Castor canadensis: The scientific name for North American beavers.

Castor fiber: The scientific name for European and Asian beavers.

Castorides: A giant ancestor of today's beavers.

dam: A type of wall built to hold back water.

fur trade: The business of buying and selling animal skins.

gland: A part of the body that produces substances such as sweat, saliva, and tears.

incisors: The four front teeth of an animal used for cutting.

kits: The name for young beavers and the young of some other fur-bearing animals.

lodge: The home of beavers, built out of sticks, rocks, and mud and located in the water.

reintroduction: Introducing again as in returning animals to areas from which they had disappeared.

rodent: A group of animals with front teeth adapted for gnawing.

silt: Small particles of sand, mud, and rock carried along by water.

wetlands: Land that has a wet and spongy soil, such as a marsh, swamp, or bog.

Books and Periodicals

Patricia Corrigan, *Beaver Magic for Kids.* Milwaukee: Gareth Stevens, 1996. Looks at the beaver's watery world and its skill in building dams and lodges.

Deborah Chase Gibson, *Beavers and Their Homes.* New York: Power Kids Press, 1999. Gives information about the physical characteristics and behaviors of beavers and their skill as builders.

Deborah Hodge, *Beavers.* Buffalo: Kids Can Press, 1998. Explores the ways that beavers build their dams and raise their young, with many diagrams and illustrations.

Andreu Llamas, *Beavers: Dam Builders.* Milwaukee: Gareth Stevens, 1996. Examines the engineering feats, physical characteristics, and behaviors of beavers.

Hope Ryden, *The Beaver.* New York: G.P. Putnam's Sons, 1986. A classic book for young readers based on the author's eighteen-month observations of wild beavers.

Paul Sterry, *Beavers and Other Rodents.* New York: TODTRI Book Publishers, 1998. Looks at the industrious beaver and their rodent relations around the world.

Time for Kids, "Eager Beavers Chomp Away at Cherry Trees," April 23, 1999. Story about beavers and the problems they caused cutting down Washington's cherry trees.

Kendra Toby, "Don't Be Fooled," *Wild,* August 1999. This story explains why beavers are rarely trapped under the trees they cut down.

Organizations to Contact

Beavers: Wetlands & Wildlife
146 Van Dyke Road
Dolgeville, NY 13329
(518) 568-2077

website: www.beaversww.org

This site provides information about beavers and help-ful hints for dealing with them.

Wildlife 2000
PO Box 6428
Denver, CO 80206
(303) 935-4995

This group provides education about beavers and help in solving beaver "problems."

Video

Beavers. Toronto: IMAX, 1988. Follows a beaver family as they construct a dam and lodge in the Canadian Rockies.

Acknowledgments

Shay Baker, Design Works 2000

Bill Berg, Minnesota Furbearer Research

John Gatz, Ohio Wesleyan University

Robert F. Gotie, New York Department of Environmental Conservation

Dan Huss, Ohio Department of Natural Resources, Division of Wildlife

Susan Langlois, Massachusetts Division of Fisheries and Wildlife

Gregory Linscomb, Louisiana Department of Wildlife and Fisheries

John Olson, Wisconsin Department of Natural Resources

Dr. David Richmond, Clayton, Idaho

Bruce H. Smith, U.S. Forest Service

Sherri Tippie, Wildlife 2000

Samara Trusso, International Association of Fish and Wildlife Agencies

Dr. John E. Becker writes children's books and magazine articles about nature and wild animals. He graduated from Ohio State University in the field of education. He has been an elementary school teacher, college professor, zoo administrator, and has worked in the field of wildlife conservation with the International Society for Endangered Cats. He currently lives in Delaware, Ohio, and teaches writing at the Thurber Writing Academy. He also enjoys visiting schools and sharing his love of writing with kids. In his spare time, Dr. Becker likes to read, hike in the woods, ice skate, and play tennis.